CORPORATE GIFTS

ALL YOU NEED TO KNOW

ANTHONY EKANEM

Contents

Preface

Corporate gifts are gifts given to employees, customers, and other stakeholders of a business. Corporate gifts may be given for different reasons. The primary function of corporate gifts is to serve as a means of thanking people for their contributions to your business. This includes thanking employees for their hard work or thanking your customers for their business. Giving people gifts to say "thank you" is a good way of ensuring repeat businesses from your customers. It will also boost the morale of your staff and other people that work with, or for, you.

Corporate gifts to clients or customers (especially those that can be used for a long time), will always remind your customers of your business, goods, or services. This will increase the chances of repeat businesses and referrals for your business.

When giving corporate gifts to customers or clients, many companies opt for small, useful items that are decorated with the company logo. By giving such items, it is possible to obtain repeat businesses, new businesses, and referrals, as the company logo can stick in the minds of those who receive the gifts. Promotional gifts are a good way to ensure that people remember you and your company when the products you sell or services you render are needed. Research has shown that such personalised corporate gifts are a good way to increase your response rates and improve your corporate profile.

Corporate gifts are under the customer service category. Giving your clients or customers gifts will not only serve to thank them for their patronage, but it will also serve as a means of building a relationship. This will bring about repeat businesses, build loyalty, and encourage them to refer you or your business to people requiring your kind of products or services. Corporate gifts are a potent marketing tool.

Good corporate gifts should show some degree of personalisation. When choosing the type of gifts to give to employees or clients, choose something they will enjoy using. Select items that are relevant to their work or personal lives, not things they might not use.

Ensure thoughtful and personalised gifts are given to people, as gift-giving in the wrong way may alienate or upset some clients, jeopardise future businesses, or diminish respect among work colleagues.

Many different items are suitable as corporate gifts. However, there are other types of gifts you can give to someone that supports your business, such as hosting a lunch in a restaurant. The type of gift you give should be well planned, with plenty of thought going into the initial decision of what to present as a corporate gift.

The appropriateness of each form of corporate gift will vary according to the workplace policy on gifts, the country your workplace is located, and other considerations.

This book will outline the steps and requirements necessary to ensure your corporate gifts are appropriate and will be well-received by the intended recipients.

CHAPTER ONE

Whom to Give Corporate Gifts

The process of choosing corporate gifts can sometimes be overwhelming. In a large company, it can be challenging to decide who should receive corporate gifts. To determine whom you will be sending corporate gifts, it is essential to decide on why you are giving the gifts and the desired response to the gift. Common reasons for giving corporate gifts include:

1. To thank clients or customers for their business, and thus ensure their loyalty and repeat businesses

2. To build a relationship with customers or business associates

3. To enhance the corporate image of your company

4. To boost staff morale and reduce employee turnover

5. To celebrate loyal customers, clients, employees, and business associates on any important achievements

6. As a means of grief or commiseration in certain circumstances

Once you have determined your reasons for giving out corporate gifts, you will be able to decide who will be receiving gifts, and thus, how many gifts will be required.

Anyone can be given a corporate gift, provided you think they are suitable recipients. The following options will help you decide whom you should give corporate gifts:

1. **Long-Term Clients and Customers:**Long-term customers or clients should receive corporate gifts. This will bring about customer loyalty and repeat businesses from the client. Giving customers corporate gifts will also increase the chances of new businesses through referrals.

2. **Business Associates:**Anyone who has participated in an important project in your organisation should be given a corporate gift as a token of your appreciation for their effort in your business.

3. **Your Boss or Executive Members:**Provided this is acceptable, and there is no company policy against it, giving your boss a corporate gift is a way of thanking them for the work and efforts they put into the company. The gifts for this category of people should appeal to their interest or hobby or should be relevant to the position they hold in the organisation.

4. **Support Staff and Colleagues:**Corporate gifts are an excellent way to show appreciation to your support staff and colleagues for their dedication and hard work. It is also a means of boosting staff morale to ensure their continued commitment and hard work. The gifts for this class of people should be functional and elegant. The gifts should provide a personalised touch and show that thought was put into the gift they have received.

5. **Individuals or Companies who provide referrals:**Many companies obtain new businesses through referrals. If your company receives a significant number of businesses via referrals from some companies or individuals, ensure you send them corporate gifts to thank them for their support for your business. This will ensure the referral of clients to your business continues.

CHAPTER TWO

The Rules for Corporate Gifts

When deciding on the corporate gifts you will be giving out, and the people you will be giving, there are some rules you should keep in mind. This is to ensure that the gifts are appropriate and will be gratefully received by the intended recipients.

The rules for giving corporate gifts vary according to the workplace and the country. The following rules are fundamental to selecting and giving corporate gifts. However, it is best to check your company's policy, as well.

1. You can freely give corporate gifts to your colleagues, employees, and support staff. However, you can only give corporate gifts to your boss if there is no company policy advising against it. In some organisations, corporate gifts to the boss may not be appropriate.

2. If you are electing to give a gift with your company's logo on it, ensure that the logo is small and stylish. If the company logo is too large, the gift will appear as a form of advertisement and will not present the intended message. Blatant advertising on a corporate gift may be offensive in some cultures and will undoubtedly diminish the desired response to the gift.

3. Avoid giving corporate gifts that touch or are applied to the skin, such as perfumes or lotions. Some gifts can be too personal and may result in some form of controversy in the office. To avoid such a situation, it is ideal to opt for a unisex present.

4. Send a card or a label with your gift to enable the recipient to know who sent the gift.

5. Choose corporate gifts with the recipients in mind. Try to send something relevant and appropriate for their work or personal life. Avoid giving gifts that the recipient cannot use. Giving thought to the choice of the gifts will ensure it is well-received by the intended recipient. Give preference to simple, thoughtful gifts, as opposed to expensive and ostentatious gifts. Ostentatious gifts will mask the meaning of what you are giving. Always ensure you maintain a standard costing for your corporate gifts.

6. Think of the corporate gifts as an investment. Therefore, ensure you select gifts that are useful and will be remembered. Bear in mind that the gifts can increase customer satisfaction, thus resulting in repeat businesses and the possibility of increased referrals to your business. Corporate gifts are also an excellent way of boosting employees' morale.

7. If you are giving perishable items as corporate gifts, ensure you include some non-perishable items too. Perishable items will only last a few days, after which they will be forgotten. Non-perishable items will last a long time and will continuously remind the recipient of your thoughtfulness. This will boost customer loyalty in your business. It will bring about repeat businesses and will also likely result in new businesses through referrals.

8. Remember that when it comes to corporate gifts, quality is far more important than quantity. A single, stylish item will be much more appreciated by the recipient than a basketful of cheap items that may not work.

CHAPTER THREE

When to Give Corporate Gifts

These days, corporate gifts are no longer only given on holidays. Corporate gifts can be given any time during the year, and for any reason. In truth, corporate gifts are often more effective when it is not given on holiday. In some countries, such as Singapore, it is traditional to give small gifts regularly.

The following list will help you determine when you should be giving out corporate gifts.

1. **To say congratulations:**If a long-term client or a member of staff just had a baby, or if someone has been promoted or made some other achievement, it is good to send them a gift to congratulate them on their success and to remind them that they are important to you.

2. **Saying goodbye:**This may be to your out-going member of staff or a long-term customer; either way, a corporate gift is an ideal way of thanking them for their contributions to your success over the years, and to let them know that they will be missed.

3. **Thanking a client for their patronage:**This is important if a significant transaction has occurred. You can send the client some form of a token to express your appreciation. The gift should be sent soon after the transaction has taken place.

4. **Major holidays:**You should aim at providing your associates, employees, and clients with corporate gifts on or around important holidays. This is the time that most competing companies will be giving corporate gifts as

well. Always ensure that the gift is well thought out and is relevant to the recipient. Major holidays include Christmas, Easter, and the New Year.

5. **To boost staff morale:**If you feel that the morale of your staff is beginning to decline, one way of boosting it is through the provision of corporate gifts to thank the employees and colleagues for their contribution to the company.

6. **As an apology:**If a situation requires an apology or some form of condolence (for example, death or tragedy of some sort), a corporate gift is an ideal means of reminding a person that they are in your thoughts.

Once you have decided to send corporate gifts, this will become a tradition that must be continued to maintain customer satisfaction, and thus, their business. For most customers, sending corporate gifts on major holidays will be sufficient for important customers, such as those who provide many referrals or customers making a large purchase, corporate gifts may be sent more often.

Remember, it is the size and importance of the business a client or associate provides that should determine the quality and type of item they receive.

CHAPTER FOUR

Different Gifts for Different Countries

The rules of giving a corporate gift will vary depending on the country in which you live, or the countries you will be doing business with. While a gift may be viewed as a pleasant gesture in some countries, in others, it may be considered a bribe.

For this reason, it is crucial to be sure you are familiar with the customs and cultures of the people with which you are dealing, as well as the policies of the companies themselves, to avoid any disturbances or insults caused by an inappropriate gift.

The following tips will help you in selecting the appropriate gifts for your business associates or clients.

1. If you are presenting a corporate gift to a Chinese client, aim to give a group gift for the company. Gifts with your company logo are acceptable. Avoid giving clocks as the word "clock" is very similar to the Chinese word for "death".

2. Gifts of alcohol, pork, or gifts made from pigskin are inappropriate gifts for a person who is of Muslim or Jewish faith.

3. It is highly inappropriate to give a corporate gift to the wife of an Arab colleague or client.

4. You are not expected to give a gift at the first meeting with clients from a Latin American background.

5. Gift giving is not expected by America, Australia, Canada, or Europe; however, it is appreciated and viewed as a nice gesture. The United States generally limits the cost of corporate gifts to no more than twenty-five Dollars.

6. Employees of a company based in Singapore are not allowed to accept corporate gifts.

7. A gift cannot be given to a Malaysian until a stable relationship has been established, as a gift given sooner may be interpreted as an attempt at bribery.

8. The exchanging of gifts is expected due to tradition in Japan, Indonesia, and the Philippines. Part of the tradition is the style in which the gifts are presented, so be sure to plan this element carefully. If you are giving a corporate gift to a Japanese associate or client, always alert them that you will be sending a gift. Do not allow it to arrive by surprise. If you are giving the gift in person, give it at the end of your visit, for the recipient to open later. Small gifts are given frequently in Indonesian culture.

9. When giving a gift in Japan or Hong Kong, be sure to present it with both hands. If the gift is presented to a client from the Middle East or Asia, only the right or both hands should be used.

10. If presenting a gift to a client or company in Singapore, do not be surprised if the gift is refused. The tradition of giving in Singapore requires the gift to be rejected three times before it can be accepted. Be prepared and remember to offer the gift three more times for its consequent acceptance.

11. Do not provide corporate presents decorated with your company logo to companies in Greece, Spain, or Portugal. This will be viewed as a blatant advertisement of your company and may be offensive to them.

12. In India, a cow is viewed as a sacred animal; for this reason; do not give gifts made of cowhide or gifts, including beef to an Indian colleague or client.

13. Those from Brazil, England, Panama, or Peru will find a dinner or meal more enjoyable than a physical gift of sorts.

CHAPTER FIVE

Types of Corporate Gifts

While considering the rules that have been mentioned in the previous chapters of this book, it is now time to select the type of corporate gifts you will be giving. There are different types of corporate gifts you can give. The kind of gift that is selected should be done with the recipient in mind. This will ensure the chosen gift is relevant and appropriate, for either their work or home life, and will be enjoyed by the recipient.

The budget allocated to corporate gifts will also play a significant role in determining the types of corporate gifts that are provided to clients, employees, and business associates.

1. **Personalised Corporate Gifts:**These types of gifts include small items, such as pens or stationery sets that are decorated with your company logo. If you are opting for a personalised corporate gift, ensure the logo is not too large, as this will appear to be a form of blatant advertising rather than a well thought out gift. Providing personalised gifts will ensure a memorable and cherished gift that will aid in reminding people of your company. Personalised gifts can help in increasing referrals for your company. Before opting for personalised corporate gifts, ensure they are a suitable choice for the recipients, as personalised corporate gifts can be looked upon as offensive in some cultures.

2. **Company Wish List:**This is a popular form of providing corporate gifts for large companies. An account is set up with a gift company, and a list of available items is sent to those who will receive the gift. The recipients are then able to choose the gift they will receive from the list. This ensures people will receive a gift that is relevant and appropriate to them and will ensure recipient satisfaction. This venture is capable of being carried out online. The company wish list is an ideal means of providing

corporate gifts to staff members to optimise staff morale.

3. **Gift Certificates:**This is an effective form of a gift if you are required to provide gifts to many people. The gift certificate is an excellent means of not discriminating between recipients and will ensure they can select a gift appropriate for them. Contact the company or merchant you will be purchasing the gift certificates from to determine the best deal they will give to you. Gift certificates are appropriate for both employees and clients alike. Bear in mind that the value of the gift certificate should vary for clients, depending on the extent of their business patronage. A client making a single purchase of one hundred Dollars may not receive a corporate gift. However, a client making multiple purchases worth thousands should be given a voucher worth a significant amount to thank them for their business, which will bring about their repeat businesses.

4. **Gift Baskets:**Gift baskets are becoming increasingly popular. As with gift vouchers, gift baskets provide an ideal means of providing a present that everyone can enjoy. Gift baskets are available with a range of different fillings, and are a nice present, as many people in the company enjoy sharing them.

5. **Wine:**Wine is only an appropriate present if you know that quality wine is enjoyment or a hobby of the recipient. Before giving wine, be sure that there is no other alternative that the recipient might be able to put to better use.

6. **Electronics:**These types of gifts are generally only selected when a small number of people will be receiving gifts. Electronic gadgets that are used for corporate gifts may include notebook computers, blackberries, or iPods. These gifts are very well received, as they can be used for personal and work situations and will last for some years.

7. **Gifts for the Office:**Gifts for the office are among the most popular types of gifts given as corporate gifts. These gifts are available in a range of processes and are a convenient option for a gift. Gifts may include pen sets, stationery sets, picture frames, and so on. Gifts for the office will ensure that the recipient has a pleasant reminder of your business each day they are in their office.

8. **Gifts for the home:**If you are selecting a gift for use in the house, be sure it is something that the recipient will be able to use for their situation. This is not a natural type of gift to select and will take some careful consideration. This gift should only be given if you know the recipient reasonably well.

9. **Services:**A popular form of corporate gift for employees of a company is the provision of a new and unique service. Services may include wireless internet access or some other type of internet package. This will aid in increasing staff morale, as well as improving effectiveness and efficiency in the workplace.

10. **Subscriptions:**This is another form of corporate gift appropriate for employees. Subscriptions that will aid in office life, such as a subscription to eFax, will provide a thoughtful gift that will make working life more relaxed and increase efficiency in the office.

11. **Dinner:**Hosting a meal in a nice restaurant is also a common form of a gift. This is an excellent means of thanking members of other companies for their support and contributions throughout the year. Hosting a meal in a restaurant will also provide an exceptional situation to build a relationship with those present.

CHAPTER SIX

Rules for Personalised Corporate Gifts

Personalised corporate gifts refer to specific items or gifts that are decorated with a company name or logo. If you decide to send out personalised corporate gifts, there are a few things you should keep in mind.

First, when deciding on the items that you will use for corporate gifts, ensure it is in some way connected to the goods or services provided by your company.

Always ensure that the items are appropriate in cost. Remember, gift items may vary according to the type and amount of business the recipient has brought to your company. The gift items should be given in line with the relationship you have with the recipient. A client who has given you a large amount of business should be rewarded with a substantial gift.

Once you have decided on the gift items, it is time to have your company logo branded on them. When deciding on the size and position of the logo, bear in mind that even though the personalised corporate gift is a means of advertising your business, it should not appear blatant. The logo should not be too big or flashy. It should be small and tasteful, and in a position to be easily noticed.

Be consistent with your giving of corporate gifts. Make corporate gifts an essential part of every sale. The gifts do not always have to be the same; they can vary each time you want to give a new gift. Just ensure a gift is given at the right time and as frequently as possible. If you do not do this, the value of the first gift you gave will diminish, and you may eventually lose a valuable colleague, partner, or client.

CHAPTER SEVEN

Choosing a Perfect Corporate Gift

So you have decided that your company should send out corporate gifts; this section will provide you with a step-by-step guide to ensure that the process of selecting and sending out your corporate gifts occurs as smoothly and efficiently as possible.

The first step is to determine when, and for what occasion, you will be sending out corporate gifts, and the response you require from your gifts. Once you have determined the occasion for the corporate gifts, you will be able to decide on who will be receiving the gifts, and how many gifts will be required. This will allow you to budget for your corporate gifts.

Once a target group has been established, and a budget has been set, it is time to select the type of corporate gift you will be providing. There are many different types of corporate gifts. The kind of gift should be chosen with careful consideration, keeping in mind the interests of the recipients. If the corporate gifts are to be sent to reliable clients, items that represent the services of a company may be selected. If the corporate gift is aimed at employees and other staff members, items that may be in some way helpful or useful in their home or work environments are most appropriate.

After selecting the items you will be giving as corporate gifts, you will be required to find a supplier capable of providing you with quality products. Be sure to obtain a quote from different suppliers to ensure you get the best price possible. Select a product of high quality; no one will be satisfied with a budget product that does not work.

Suppliers can be sourced using the yellow pages or another directory. Many suppliers now offer their services online, allowing for a straightforward process for purchasing gifts. If multiple forms of gifts or various suppliers are required, it may be useful allocating the job of obtaining the corporate gifts to one or two people. This will ensure that the job is done as efficiently and effectively as possible. Most gift suppliers will be able to wrap and deliver the gifts to the appropriate recipients.

If the gift suppliers are not delivering the gifts to their desired locations, you will have to have them delivered to your place of work where they will subsequently be delivered to the appropriate recipients.

Remember to include appropriate notes with the gifts to ensure the recipients know the source of the gift.

CHAPTER EIGHT

Save Time – Buy Gifts Online

Advancement in technology has seen the process of selecting and purchasing corporate gifts become increasingly easier. Many gift suppliers are now able to offer their services online, which makes the process of choosing and buying corporate gifts very easy.

The following steps will provide you with an overview of how to select and buy your corporate gifts online:

1. Begin by deciding who will be the recipients of corporate gifts from your company, and how many gifts you will be required to provide. Once you have determined the number of gifts to buy, you will also have to determine the types of gifts to buy. There are different types of corporate gifts available. Ensure that the gifts you choose are appropriate to the recipients and will be something they will use in their home or their work life.

2. Visit the online yellow pages, or an online directory, and search for relevant gift providers in your local area. While gift providers in your local area are generally easiest to deal with and will be able to hand-deliver the gifts, you are also able to purchase gifts from almost anywhere in the world. Select a company that best suits your needs. Compare prices of different companies to ensure you obtain the best price possible.

3. Place order for the relevant type and number of items and fill in all relevant details. Most online gift merchants will have facilities to allow you to pay for the order in one transaction online. This transaction will occur during the ordering process. You will be required to provide credit card details for payment. If possible, try to use a company account for

your purchase, as the items may be tax-deductible.

CHAPTER NINE

The Pros and Cons of Corporate Gifts

Before deciding to send out corporate gifts, it is important to be aware of the pros and cons associated with the process. If the process of giving corporate gifts is carried out correctly, the gift can bring benefits to the company. This is particularly true if the gift is something that the recipient can keep for a long time and can use on a repeated basis.

If these gifts can have a small logo emblazoned upon them, you will be able to provide your patrons with a daily reminder of your company and the service you provide. This proves to be particularly beneficial in increasing the chances of repeat business and increasing the number of referrals for your company.

Corporate gifts are flexible, and it is possible to find a variety of different gifts to suit a variety of different budgets. Just about any item can be used as a corporate gift; however, it is often best to select an item that represents your company's service in some way.

As mentioned above, many of these gifts can be decorated with a small company logo, which makes the gift a marketing tool.

Corporate gifts also help increase customer loyalty. Studies have shown that corporate gift is an effective means of boosting response rates and raising the profile of your company.

There are a few disadvantages that may come from giving corporate gifts. However, these can generally be avoided by ensuring the process of selecting and providing the gifts is done correctly and with care.

Depending on the item selected, there may be limitations as to the colours and types of printing on the item. This may limit how you may print your company logo on the item. These restrictions are generally able to be worked around to change how the log is printed, or perhaps even select a different type of item to be used as the corporate gift.

If you have opted for a customised corporate present, it is also important to remember that it takes time to have the corporate gifts manufactured and delivered. Periods will vary depending on the item selected and the printing required and can range from a few days to a few weeks. Allow extra time during major holidays, as suppliers are generally at their busiest during these periods.

If you opt to select and purchase your gifts online, you run the risk of securing goods that are not of the quality you were expecting, as you will be unable to inspect the goods before purchase. It may be best to search for suppliers online and check the quality of products itself before making your purchase.

At the very least, it is recommended to order a sample for yourself to ensure that the quality meets your needs.

www.ingramcontent.com/pod-product-compliance
Lightning Source LLC
Chambersburg PA
CBHW061523180526
45171CB00001B/308